The World We All Want

The World We All Want

A course on how the Bible really works

Tim Chester and Steve Timmis

Authentic

11 10 09 08 07 06 05   7 6 5 4 3 2 1

First published in 2005 by Authentic Media
9 Holdom Avenue, Bletchley, Milton Keynes, Bucks, MK1 1QR, UK
and 129 Mobilization Drive, Waynesboro, GA 30830-4575, USA
www.authenticmedia.co.uk

British Library Cataloguing in Publication Data
A catalogue record for this book is available from the British Library

ISBN 1-85078-636-4

Cover design by fourninezero design.
Typeset by Temple Design
Print Management by Adare Carwin
Printed by J. H. Haynes & Co. Ltd., Sparkford

We all dream of a better world

We all dream of a better world – a world of security, plenty and friendship. Christians believe that God promises just such a new world. The Bible is the story of what God had done and what he will do to keep that promise.

The World We All Want is for people who are interested in the message of the Bible. It is an introduction to the Bible story – the story Christians believe to be the story of our world and its future.

You can use the course on your own, with a friend or as a group. The advantage of doing it with a Christian is that they can answer your questions. Each session looks at some passages from the Bible. This is the most important part of the course. It is an opportunity for you to find out for yourself what the Bible actually says. There is also a section of the Bible to read in preparation for the next session if you want although you do not have to.

The course starts at the end of the story with God's promise of a new world. It then moves to the centre of the story – to the point in history when we get a glimpse of God's new world. And then it goes back to the beginning and works through to the point in the story where we are today. The diagrams show the story in its proper sequence. This means the diagrams are numbered differently from the sessions.

Contents

SESSION ONE 1
God promises the world we all want
Revelation chapters 21–22 and Mark chapter 5

SESSION TWO 11
Jesus shows us God's new world
Mark chapters 4–5 and Mark chapter 8

SESSION THREE 23
We have spoiled God's good world
Genesis chapters 1–3

SESSION FOUR 33
God promises a new world
Genesis chapters 12 and 15 and Romans chapter 4

SESSION FIVE 43
We cannot create God's new world
Nehemiah chapter 9 and Ezekiel chapter 36

SESSION SIX 57
We can enjoy God's new world because of Jesus
Mark chapters 15–16

SESSION SEVEN 67
**Christians are God's people waiting
for God's new world**
Acts chapters 1–2

FOR LEADERS 77

FURTHER READING 83

SESSION ONE

God promises
the world we all want

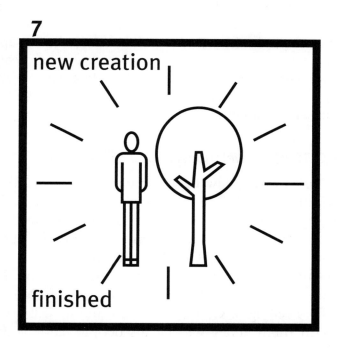

God promises the world we all want.

We know this promise is real because there

was a point in history when we glimpsed the

world we all want.

1. What kind of a world would you like to live in?

draw a world - all contribute

Everybody's idea of a perfect world is different. Some people would play football all the time. Other people would ban it. But when we think about it seriously there are common themes to our dreams. There is a world we all want. It's a world without poverty – a world of plenty and provision. It's a world without pollution and the threat of global warming. It's a place where we don't grow old and where we never lose those we love. It's a place where we're not hurt by other people and we don't hurt them. The Bible tells us that there is such a world.

BIBLE EXTRACT: Revelation, chapter 21, verses 1–5

A vision

Then I saw a new heaven and a new earth, for the first heaven and the first earth had passed away, and there was no longer any sea. ² I saw the Holy City, the new Jerusalem, coming down out of heaven from God, prepared as a bride beautifully dressed for her husband. ³ And I heard a loud voice from the throne saying, 'Now the dwelling of God is with men, and he will live with them. They will be his people, and God himself will be with them and be their God. ⁴ He

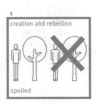

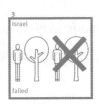
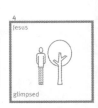

will wipe every tear from their eyes. There will be no more death or mourning or crying or pain, for the old order of things has passed away.'

⁵ He who was seated on the throne said, 'I am making everything new!' Then he said, 'Write this down, for these words are trustworthy and true.'

2. What is this new world like?

- 'new' ie completely different
- all the things we hate are gone

3. What surprises you about this new world?

- it doesn't exist yet
- no sea - bride etc
- things it doesn't mention

This description uses picture language. The sea represents a source of threat, so a world without a sea was a world of security (verse 1). Jerusalem is God's city and the bride is a picture of God's special relationship with his people. God promises that people will know him and live in his new world.

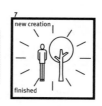

3

4. *Who is at the centre of this new world?*

God - speaking & putting new world into action - what makes it so completely different is that God is living with his people

In the present we are at the centre of our world. We live our lives without God. But three times in verse 3 we are told that in this new world God will be with his people. Having God looking over your shoulder might not seem good news but, as we will discover, God with his people is actually the world we all want.

list things we don't like about world - trace back to prob of sin - (i... without God

BIBLE EXTRACT: Revelation, chapter 22, verses 1–6

more the about the new world

Then the angel showed me the river of the water of life, as clear as crystal, flowing from the throne of God and of the Lamb ² down the middle of the great street of the city. On each side of the river stood the tree of life, bearing twelve crops of fruit, yielding its fruit every month. And the leaves of the tree are for the healing of the nations. ³ No longer will there be any curse. The throne of God and of the Lamb will be in the city, and his servants will serve him. ⁴ They will see his face, and his name will be on their foreheads. ⁵ There will be no more night. They will not need the light of a lamp or the light of the sun, for the Lord God will give them light. And they will reign for ever and ever.

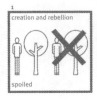
1 creation and rebellion / spoiled

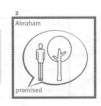
2 Abraham / promised

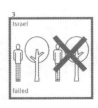
3 Israel / failed

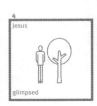
4 Jesus / glimpsed

⁶ The angel said to me, 'These words are trustworthy and true. The Lord, the God of the spirits of the prophets, sent his angel to show his servants the things that must soon take place.'

5. What is this new world like?

- water of life, tree of life → imagery describing life to its fulness
- no night / darkness
- no curse - explaining later - God isn't against us

6. What surprises you about this new world?

- lasts for ever
- will 'soon take place'

God promises a new world – the world we all want. The Bible paints an attractive and compelling picture of this world for us.

7. What does the writer say about these words of promise in Revelation 21:5 and 22:6?

- we can trust the writer - esp if we trust John's gospel
- 'trustworthy & true' – God's promise

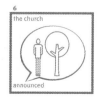

This new world is not going to come about because of revolutionaries, business people, politicians or philosophers. The Bible claims that only God can bring this wonderful new world into existence. God says these words of promise are 'trustworthy and true'.

But it sounds too good to be true. How can we be sure? The answer is that there was a time when we glimpsed the world we all want. There was a time in history when God's new world existed.

BIBLE EXTRACT: Mark, chapter 5, verses 21–43

When Jesus had again crossed over by boat to the other side of the lake, a large crowd gathered round him. ²² While he was by the lake, one of the synagogue rulers, named Jairus, came there. Seeing Jesus, he fell at his feet ²³ and pleaded earnestly with him, 'My little daughter is dying. Please come and put your hands on her so that she will be healed and live.' ²⁴ So Jesus went with him.

A large crowd followed and pressed around him. ²⁵ And a woman was there who had been subject to bleeding for twelve years. ²⁶ She had suffered a great deal under the care of many doctors and had spent all she had, yet instead of getting better she grew worse. ²⁷ When she heard about Jesus, she came up behind him in the crowd and touched his cloak, ²⁸ because she thought, 'If I just touch his clothes, I will be

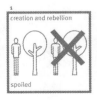
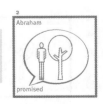
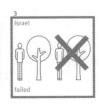

healed.' ²⁹ Immediately her bleeding stopped and she felt in her body that she was freed from her suffering.

³⁰ At once Jesus realised that power had gone out from him. He turned around in the crowd and asked, 'Who touched my clothes?'

³¹ 'You see the people crowding against you,' his disciples answered, 'and yet you can ask, "Who touched me?"'

³² But Jesus kept looking around to see who had done it. ³³ Then the woman, knowing what had happened to her, came and fell at his feet and, trembling with fear, told him the whole truth. ³⁴ He said to her, 'Daughter, your faith has healed you. Go in peace and be freed from your suffering.'

³⁵ While Jesus was still speaking, some men came from the house of Jairus, the synagogue ruler. 'Your daughter is dead,' they said. 'Why bother the teacher any more?'

³⁶ Ignoring what they said, Jesus told the synagogue ruler, 'Don't be afraid; just believe.'

³⁷ He did not let anyone follow him except Peter, James and John the brother of James. ³⁸ When they came to the home of the synagogue ruler,

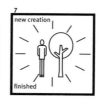

Jesus saw a commotion, with people crying and wailing loudly. [39] He went in and said to them, 'Why all this commotion and wailing? The child is not dead but asleep.' [40] But they laughed at him.

After he put them all out, he took the child's father and mother and the disciples who were with him, and went in where the child was. [41] He took her by the hand and said to her, '*Talitha koum!*' (which means, 'Little girl, I say to you, get up!'). [42] Immediately the girl stood up and walked around (she was twelve years old). At this they were completely astonished. [43] He gave strict orders not to let anyone know about this, and told them to give her something to eat.

This book of the Bible is not talking about something that may happen in the future. It is describing something that has already happened in history. It was written by a man called Mark who knew people who had seen these events and probably saw some of them himself. Mark tells us about a man called Jesus who lived about 2,000 years ago.

8. *What does Mark show us about Jesus?*

- he cares, is powerful to heal & raise from the dead
- can act outside limitations of this world

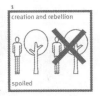
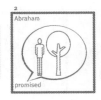

9. **We have read about a world with 'no more death or mourning or crying or pain'. How do we see a glimpse of God's new world in these verses?**

girl raised from dead
family stop mourning & crying
woman healed from pain & bleeding

Mark tells about a woman who was ill. In her world her condition meant that she would have been an outcast. And there seemed to be no hope of cure (verses 25–26). But Jesus changes everything (verses 29 and 34). Mark goes on to tell us of a young girl who is raised from death. Jesus simply speaks to her and she comes back to life (verses 41–42). The mourning and crying stop.

It was only a glimpse of God's new world. Even as Jesus was giving life back to the girl, thousands of other people in the world were dying. So the world we all want did not exist fully. But it was the real thing. It was as though a curtain was pulled back and we were allowed to see a glimpse of that world. If what Jesus did was real then God's new world is not just a dream.

10. **The Bible says God promises a new world. What difference do you think this should make to life now?**

- gives hope - able to endure the present life

- knowing Jesus now prepares us for it - he changes us to family likeness

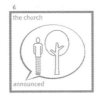
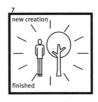

5 the cross achieved

6 the church announced

7 new creation finished

SUMMARY

God promises the world we all want. He promises:

- a people who know God (represented in the diagrams by a person)
- that we will enjoy a new world (represented in the diagrams by a tree)

We can trust this promise because Jesus gave us a glimpse of God's new world.

BACKGROUND READING FOR THE NEXT SESSION

Mark, chapter 4, verse 35 to chapter 5, verse 43

Jesus shows us God's new world

4

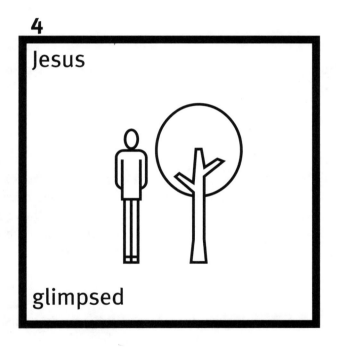

Jesus

glimpsed

Jesus had the power to make God's new world.
But Jesus said it was necessary for him to die
so we could enjoy it.

In our last session we spent some time dreaming together. We dreamed of a new world – a world of peace and provision without tears or suffering. It is a world without fear.

1. *What makes you afraid?*

Spiders, illness, ghosts, death, ~~ear~~ volcanoes, etc

2. *What would we have to put right to enjoy the world we all want?*

So - none of these things will be in the world we all want.

Do you remember

In the Bible God promises a new world. And in the life of Jesus we are given a glimpse of God's new world. It is as if we have been able to sneak into the kitchen and taste a mouthful of the cooking. We have had a foretaste of a great feast. We see, too, in the life of Jesus that he has the power to create God's new world.

BIBLE EXTRACT: Mark, chapter 4, verses 35–41

That day when evening came, Jesus said to his disciples, 'Let us go over to the other side.'

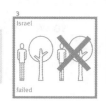
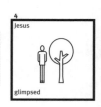

³⁶ Leaving the crowd behind, they took him along, just as he was, in the boat. There were also other boats with him. ³⁷ A furious squall came up, and the waves broke over the boat, so that it was nearly swamped. ³⁸ Jesus was in the stern, sleeping on a cushion. The disciples woke him and said to him, 'Teacher, don't you care if we drown?'

³⁹ He got up, rebuked the wind and said to the waves, 'Quiet! Be still!' Then the wind died down and it was completely calm. ⁴⁰ He said to his disciples, 'Why are you so afraid? Do you still have no faith?'

⁴¹ They were terrified and asked each other, 'Who is this? Even the wind and the waves obey him!'

This is a situation where there is fear?
Who is afraid + what of?

3. What does Jesus rescue his followers from in verses 35–41?

who

Power of nature.

Now look at another example of J sorting out the things that make us afraid.

BIBLE EXTRACT: Mark, chapter 5, verses 1–20

They went across the lake to the region of the Gerasenes. ² When Jesus got out of the boat, a

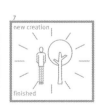

man with an evil spirit came from the tombs to meet him. ³ This man lived in the tombs, and no-one could bind him any more, not even with a chain. ⁴ For he had often been chained hand and foot, but he tore the chains apart and broke the irons on his feet. No-one was strong enough to subdue him. ⁵ Night and day among the tombs and in the hills he would cry out and cut himself with stones.

⁶ When he saw Jesus from a distance, he ran and fell on his knees in front of him. ⁷ He shouted at the top of his voice, 'What do you want with me, Jesus, Son of the Most High God? Swear to God that you won't torture me!' ⁸ For Jesus had said to him, 'Come out of this man, you evil spirit!'

⁹ Then Jesus asked him, 'What is your name?'

'My name is Legion,' he replied, 'for we are many.' ¹⁰ And he begged Jesus again and again not to send them out of the area.

¹¹ A large herd of pigs was feeding on the nearby hillside. ¹² The demons begged Jesus, 'Send us among the pigs; allow us to go into them.' ¹³ He gave them permission, and the evil spirits came out and went into the pigs. The herd, about two thousand in number, rushed down the steep bank into the lake and were drowned.

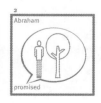
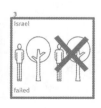
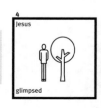

¹⁴ Those tending the pigs ran off and reported this in the town and countryside, and the people went out to see what had happened. ¹⁵ When they came to Jesus, they saw the man who had been possessed by the legion of demons, sitting there, dressed and in his right mind; and they were afraid. ¹⁶ Those who had seen it told the people what had happened to the demon-possessed man – and told about the pigs as well. ¹⁷ Then the people began to plead with Jesus to leave their region.

¹⁸ As Jesus was getting into the boat, the man who had been demon-possessed begged to go with him. ¹⁹ Jesus did not let him, but said, 'Go home to your family and tell them how much the Lord has done for you, and how he has had mercy on you.' ²⁰ So the man went away and began to tell in the Decapolis how much Jesus had done for him. And all the people were amazed.

4. What do verses 1–20 show about the power of Jesus?

This is really scary stuff – chains couldn't hold the man
Who is more powerful? Jesus or the spirit? Vote
Which verses show this?
– Instantly recognises J for who he is ✓ 7
– knows J had power to torture spirit ✓ 7
– Begged J v10 + 12 – showed J in charge (+ v13)

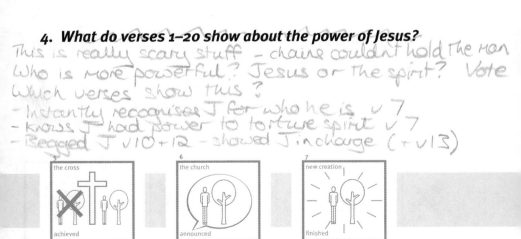

5 the cross — achieved
6 the church — announced
7 new creation — finished

Do you remember last week — *bleeding woman* — *Jairus' daughter* / *the girl who died*

Recap stories

Who had power to heal both of them ↓

what did Jesus he have power over?

BIBLE EXTRACT: Mark, chapter 5, verses 21–43

When Jesus had again crossed over by boat to the other side of the lake, a large crowd gathered round him while he was by the lake. ²² Then one of the synagogue rulers, named Jairus, came there. Seeing Jesus, he fell at his feet ²³ and pleaded earnestly with him, 'My little daughter is dying. Please come and put your hands on her so that she will be healed and live.' ²⁴ So Jesus went with him.

A large crowd followed and pressed around him. ²⁵ And a woman was there who had been subject to bleeding for twelve years. ²⁶ She had suffered a great deal under the care of many doctors and had spent all she had, yet instead of getting better she grew worse. ²⁷ When she heard about Jesus, she came up behind him in the crowd and touched his cloak, ²⁸ because she thought, 'If I just touch his clothes, I will be healed.' ²⁹ Immediately her bleeding stopped and she felt in her body that she was freed from her suffering.

³⁰ At once Jesus realised that power had gone out from him. He turned around in the crowd and asked, 'Who touched my clothes?'

³¹ 'You see the people crowding against you,' his disciples answered, 'and yet you can ask, "Who touched me?"'

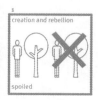
creation and rebellion
spoiled

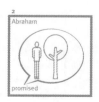
Abraham
promised

Israel
failed

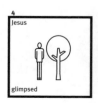
Jesus
glimpsed

³² But Jesus kept looking around to see who had done it. ³³ Then the woman, knowing what had happened to her, came and fell at his feet and, trembling with fear, told him the whole truth. ³⁴ He said to her, 'Daughter, your faith has healed you. Go in peace and be freed from your suffering.'

³⁵ While Jesus was still speaking, some men came from the house of Jairus, the synagogue ruler. 'Your daughter is dead,' they said. 'Why bother the teacher any more?'

³⁶ Ignoring what they said, Jesus told the synagogue ruler, 'Don't be afraid; just believe.'

³⁷ He did not let anyone follow him except Peter, James and John the brother of James. ³⁸ When they came to the home of the synagogue ruler, Jesus saw a commotion, with people crying and wailing loudly. ³⁹ He went in and said to them, 'Why all this commotion and wailing? The child is not dead but asleep.' ⁴⁰ But they laughed at him.

After he put them all out, he took the child's father and mother and the disciples who were with him, and went in where the child was. ⁴¹ He took her by the hand and said to her, '*Talitha koum!*' (which means, 'Little girl, I say to you, get up!'). ⁴² Immediately the girl stood up and

walked around (she was twelve years old). At this they were completely astonished. ⁴³ He gave strict orders not to let anyone know about this, and told them to give her something to eat.

5. What do verses 21–43 show about the power of Jesus?

Over sickne

6. In 4:41 the followers of Jesus ask 'Who is this?' Who does Mark think Jesus is? Who do you think Jesus is?

read

7. What does Jesus expect from people (see Mark 4:40; 5:34 and 5:36)?

Faith / believe

1 creation and rebellion

spoiled

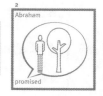

2 Abraham

promised

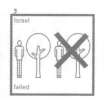

3 Israel

failed

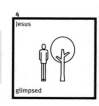

4 Jesus

glimpsed

We have seen that Jesus has power:

- over nature
- over the spirit world
- over sickness
- over death

Do you know story of feeding of 5000?

Mark also tells us that Jesus fed thousands of hungry people with a handful of food (see Mark 6:33–44 and 8:1–10). Jesus has power over all the things that threaten us and spoil our lives. So if what Mark is saying is true, then Jesus has the power to create God's new world.

Jesus expects people to trust him. He wants us to believe that he can create God's new world. Jesus wants us to have faith instead of fear (see Mark 4:40; 5:33–34 and 5:36).

But what happens to J?

But there is a big surprise: Jesus himself dies. The man who defeated death becomes its victim. It seems as if our hopes have been built up only to be shattered. Is this the end of hope for God's new world?

BIBLE EXTRACT: Mark, chapter 8, verses 31–33

> Jesus then began to teach them that the Son of Man must suffer many things and be rejected by the elders, chief priests and teachers of the law, and that he must be killed and after three days rise again. ³² He spoke plainly about this, and Peter took him aside and began to rebuke him.

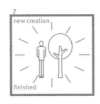

³³ But when Jesus turned and looked at his disciples, he rebuked Peter. 'Out of my sight, Satan!' he said. 'You do not have in mind the things of God, but the things of men.'

The Son of Man is how Jesus often talks about himself. Peter was one of the friends of Jesus.

8. What does Jesus tell his friends?

9. What is Peter's response to what Jesus says?

Jesus tells his friends ahead of time that he is going to die. But he also tells them that he must die.

Surely it would be better for Jesus to go on healing the sick, defeating evil spirits and feeding the hungry. Why must this good man die? But Jesus says that we do not see things as God sees them. The death of Jesus is part of God's plan. The Bible tells us that Jesus died so that we could enjoy God's new world. The rest of the course shows us why.

Does anyone know why Jesus died? Link in The pic of Gods new world

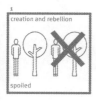
1 creation and rebellion / spoiled

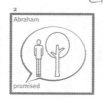
2 Abraham / promised

3 Israel / failed

4 Jesus / glimpsed

10. *What do you make of Jesus?*

SUMMARY

Jesus had the power to make God's new world. But Jesus said it was necessary for him to die so that we could enjoy that new world.

Draw picture.

BACKGROUND READING FOR THE NEXT SESSION

Genesis chapters 1–3

World is very interested in the supernatural - things that heal you, magic powers (Harry Potter) etc

Superheroes

What powers would your superhero have?

Pics superheroes

do their powers match Jesus'?

Spiderman
Superman
Bananaman
~~Wonderwoman~~.
The Incredibles

Jesus is the ultimate answer to all healings/powers etc

5
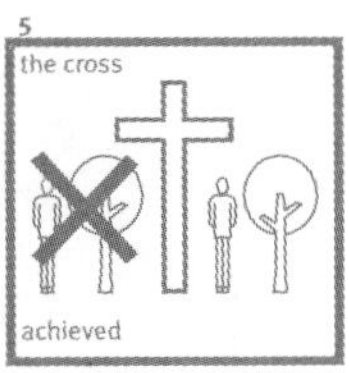
the cross
achieved

6
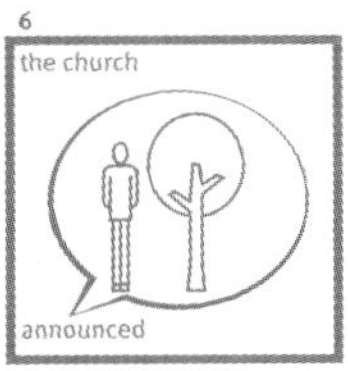
the church
announced

7
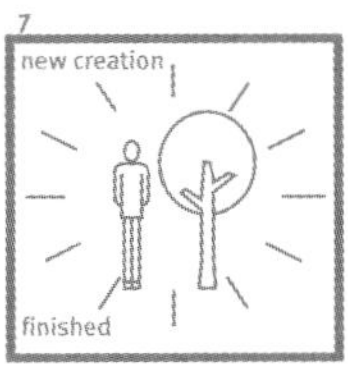
new creation
finished

SESSION THREE

We have spoiled God's good world

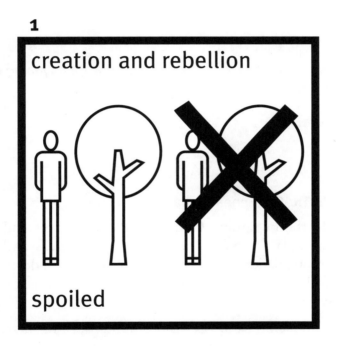

1

creation and rebellion

spoiled

We have spoiled the good world that God made, but God promises someone who will put it right.

God promises a new world – the world we all want. And we have had a glimpse of that world in the life of Jesus.

1. *Do you think the world is basically good or basically bad?*

– write & read out stories

2. *What do you think are the biggest problems facing the world today?*

BIBLE EXTRACT: Genesis, chapter 1, verses 1–5

¹In the beginning God created the heavens and the earth. ² Now the earth was formless and empty, darkness was over the surface of the deep, and the Spirit of God was hovering over the waters.

³ And God said, 'Let there be light,' and there was light. ⁴ God saw that the light was good, and he separated the light from the darkness. ⁵ God

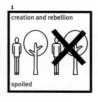
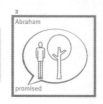

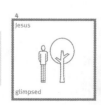

called the light 'day', and the darkness he called 'night'. And there was evening, and there was morning – the first day.

3. What does God think of the world he made?

BIBLE EXTRACT: Genesis, chapter 2, verses 8–9 and 15–17

Now the LORD God had planted a garden in the east, in Eden; and there he put the man he had formed. ⁹ And the LORD God made all kinds of trees grow out of the ground – trees that were pleasing to the eye and good for food. In the middle of the garden were the tree of life and the tree of the knowledge of good and evil …The LORD God took the man and put him in the Garden of Eden to work it and take care of it. ¹⁶ And the LORD God commanded the man, 'You are free to eat from any tree in the garden; ¹⁷ but you must not eat from the tree of the knowledge of good and evil, for when you eat of it you will surely die.'

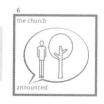
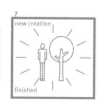

4. *What is the home God made for mankind like?*

God is the one who made all things and controls all things. He made the world by speaking his word. And God made a good world – a place of beauty, security and plenty. *'God saw all that he had made, and it was very good'* (Genesis 1:31). This is the world we all want. We were made to enjoy relationships with one another, with the world around us and above all with God himself.

But the world we know is full of evil, pain and division. So what went wrong?

BIBLE EXTRACT: Genesis, chapter 3, verses 1–7

> Now the serpent was more crafty than any of the wild animals the LORD God had made. He said to the woman, 'Did God really say, "You must not eat from any tree in the garden"?'
>
> ² The woman said to the serpent, 'We may eat fruit from the trees in the garden, ³ but God did say, "You must not eat fruit from the tree that is in the middle of the garden, and you must not touch it, or you will die."'

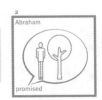
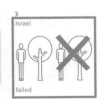

⁴ 'You will not surely die,' the serpent said to the woman. ⁵ 'For God knows that when you eat of it your eyes will be opened, and you will be like God, knowing good and evil.'

⁶ When the woman saw that the fruit of the tree was good for food and pleasing to the eye, and also desirable for gaining wisdom, she took some and ate it. She also gave some to her husband, who was with her, and he ate it. ⁷ Then the eyes of both of them were opened, and they realised that they were naked; so they sewed fig leaves together and made coverings for themselves.

The Bible says that the serpent represents Satan. Satan is an angel or spirit who rejected God and became God's enemy.

5. What was life like under God's rule?

6. How does the serpent portray God's rule?

7. What does the serpent suggest about God's word?

God's rule was a rule of love, peace, freedom and security. But the serpent portrays God's rule as oppressive. And the serpent suggests God's word cannot be trusted.

8. Why was eating the fruit such a bad thing to do?

There was nothing magical about the fruit. The significance of eating the fruit was that by doing so we rejected God's rule. We would not let God be God. 'Knowing good and evil' does not mean finding out some things are wrong, because Adam had already been told not to eat the fruit (Genesis 2:16–17). Nor does it mean experiencing evil, because the perfect God knows good and evil (Genesis 3:22). 'Knowing good and evil' means deciding for ourselves what is right and wrong (verse 5). We want to run our lives our way instead of God's way. We are like this because of what the first man and woman did. They were our representatives. The reason this world is not the world we all want is because each of us contributes to its brokenness. We have rejected God's world and chosen to live our own way. There is a sense in which this broken world is the world we have chosen.

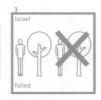

9. *What do you think the world would be like if evil was never punished?*

BIBLE EXTRACT: Genesis, chapter 3, verses 14–24

So the LORD God said to the serpent, 'Because you have done this, cursed are you above all the livestock and all the wild animals! You will crawl on your belly and you will eat dust all the days of your life. ¹⁵ And I will put enmity between you and the woman, and between your offspring and hers; he will crush your head, and you will strike his heel.'

¹⁶ To the woman he said, 'I will greatly increase your pains in childbearing; with pain you will give birth to children. Your desire will be for your husband, and he will rule over you.'

¹⁷ To Adam he said, 'Because you listened to your wife and ate from the tree about which I commanded you, "You must not eat of it," cursed is the ground because of you; through painful toil you will eat of it all the days of your life. ¹⁸ It will produce thorns and thistles for you, and you will

eat the plants of the field. [19] By the sweat of your brow you will eat your food until you return to the ground, since from it you were taken; for dust you are and to dust you will return.'

[20] Adam named his wife Eve, because she would become the mother of all the living.

[21] The LORD God made garments of skin for Adam and his wife and clothed them. [22] And the LORD God said, 'The man has now become like one of us, knowing good and evil. He must not be allowed to reach out his hand and take also from the tree of life and eat, and live for ever.' [23] So the LORD God banished him from the Garden of Eden to work the ground from which he had been taken. [24] After he drove the man out, he placed on the east side of the Garden of Eden cherubim and a flaming sword flashing back and forth to guard the way to the tree of life.

10. How does God respond to humanity's rejection of him?

God says the world is now cursed (verses 17–19). We are now separated from God (verses 22–24). We have become God's

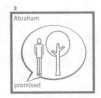
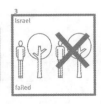

enemies and we have spoiled the world. As a result we all face God's judgment. We face physical death and spiritual death – separation from the goodness and love of God. Instead of the world we want, we get the world we deserve. We do not live in the world we all want because we are not the people we ought to be.

The Bible's account of the world explains why the world contains both good things and bad things. God made the world good and we still see in our world beauty, kindness and happiness. But we have spoiled God's good world and so we also see ugliness, evil and suffering. The Bible helps us to make sense of this paradox.

11. What does God promise in Genesis 3:15?

God promises someone who will put right what we have done. One of the descendants of Eve will crush Satan (though he will have to suffer – Satan will 'strike his heel'). Satan has spoiled God's world. But God promises a rescuer who will defeat Satan and restore God's good world.

12. Do you think of yourself as a good person or a bad person?

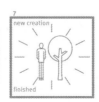

SUMMARY

We have spoiled the good world that God made and God will judge us. But God promises someone who will put it right.

BACKGROUND READING FOR THE NEXT SESSION

Genesis, chapters 12 and 15

SESSION FOUR

God promises a new world

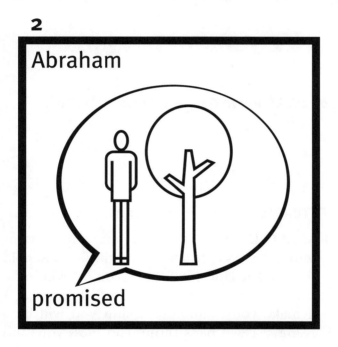

God promises a people who know God and
a land of plenty and security.

In the last session we saw that we have rejected God. As a result:

- we have become God's enemies
- we have spoiled God's world

But God did not leave things like this.

1. Do you think we can have a relationship with God?

2. If you could talk to God, what would you say?

BIBLE EXTRACT: Genesis, chapter 12, verses 1–7

> The LORD had said to Abram, 'Leave your country, your people and your father's household and go to the land I will show you. ² I will make you into a great nation and I will bless you; I will make your name great, and you will be a blessing. ³ I will bless those who bless you, and whoever curses you I will curse; and all peoples on earth will be blessed through you.'

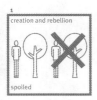
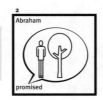
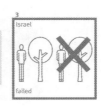
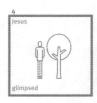

⁴ So Abram left, as the LORD had told him; and Lot went with him. Abram was seventy-five years old when he set out from Haran. ⁵ He took his wife Sarai, his nephew Lot, all the possessions they had accumulated and the people they had acquired in Haran, and they set out for the land of Canaan, and they arrived there.

⁶ Abram travelled through the land as far as the site of the great tree of Moreh at Shechem. The Canaanites were then in the land, ⁷ but the LORD appeared to Abram and said, 'To your offspring I will give this land.' So he built an altar there to the LORD, who had appeared to him.

3. What does God promise to Abram?

4. We have become God's enemies and spoiled God's world. How does the promise to Abram put right these problems?

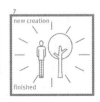

God promises a nation or a people (verse 2). Abram is later renamed 'Abraham' which means 'father of many' because he will be the beginning of God's new people. We have become God's enemies, but now God promises a people who will know God and be his people. We can be God's friends.

God also promises Abraham a land (verse 7). We spoiled God's good world, but now God promises a land of plenty and security. The Bible often describes it as a place of 'rest' (see, for example, Deuteronomy 12:7–10; Joshua 21:43–44; 1 Kings 8:56–57).

Our rebellion brought a curse. Now God says blessing will come through Abraham's family. God's promised rescuer will be one of Abraham's descendants.

5. Who will benefit from the blessing promised to Abraham?

God focuses in on one man. But God chooses Abraham for the sake of all nations. God says that he will bless all peoples through Abraham's descendants.

BIBLE EXTRACT: Genesis, chapter 12, verses 10–20

> Now there was a famine in the land, and Abram went down to Egypt to live there for a while

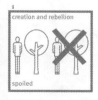
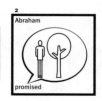
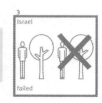

because the famine was severe. ¹¹ As he was about to enter Egypt, he said to his wife Sarai, 'I know what a beautiful woman you are. ¹² When the Egyptians see you, they will say, "This is his wife." Then they will kill me but will let you live. ¹³ Say you are my sister, so that I will be treated well for your sake and my life will be spared because of you.'

¹⁴ When Abram came to Egypt, the Egyptians saw that she was a very beautiful woman. ¹⁵ And when Pharaoh's officials saw her, they praised her to Pharaoh, and she was taken into his palace. ¹⁶ He treated Abram well for her sake, and Abram acquired sheep and cattle, male and female donkeys, menservants and maidservants, and camels.

¹⁷ But the LORD inflicted serious diseases on Pharaoh and his household because of Abram's wife Sarai. ¹⁸ So Pharaoh summoned Abram. 'What have you done to me?' he said. 'Why didn't you tell me she was your wife? ¹⁹ Why did you say, "She is my sister," so that I took her to be my wife? Now then, here is your wife. Take her and go!' ²⁰ Then Pharaoh gave orders about Abram to his men, and they sent him on his way, with his wife and everything he had.

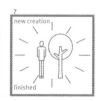

6. What effect does Abraham have on the nation of Egypt?

The problem with a new world is this: it would be okay until you put people in it! We end up spoiling things. Instead of bringing blessing to the nations, Abraham brings a curse. If we are to be God's people and enjoy God's new world then God must deal with our rebellion and his judgment.

7. When someone makes you a promise, what kind of response do they usually want from you?

BIBLE EXTRACT: Genesis, chapter 15, verses 1–7

> After this, the word of the LORD came to Abram in a vision: 'Do not be afraid, Abram. I am your shield, your very great reward.'
>
> ² But Abram said, 'O Sovereign LORD, what can you give me since I remain childless and the one who will inherit my estate is Eliezer of Damascus?' ³ And Abram said, 'You have given

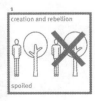
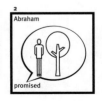
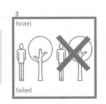
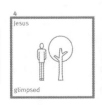

me no children; so a servant in my household will be my heir.'

⁴ Then the word of the LORD came to him: 'This man will not be your heir, but a son coming from your own body will be your heir.' ⁵ He took him outside and said, 'Look up at the heavens and count the stars – if indeed you can count them.' Then he said to him, 'So shall your offspring be.'

⁶ Abram believed the LORD, and he credited it to him as righteousness.

⁷ He also said to him, 'I am the LORD, who brought you out of Ur of the Chaldeans to give you this land to take possession of it.'

8. What does God promise to Abraham?

9. How does Abraham respond?

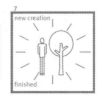

Abraham responds to God's promise with faith (verse 6). This helps to see what faith is: faith is trusting in the promises of God.

BIBLE EXTRACT: Romans, chapter 4, verses 1–8

What then shall we say that Abraham, our forefather, discovered in this matter? [2] If, in fact, Abraham was justified by works, he had something to boast about – but not before God. [3] What does the Scripture say? 'Abraham believed God, and it was credited to him as righteousness.'

[4] Now when a man works, his wages are not credited to him as a gift, but as an obligation. [5] However, to the man who does not work but trusts God who justifies the wicked, his faith is credited as righteousness. [6] David says the same thing when he speaks of the blessedness of the man to whom God credits righteousness apart from works:

[7] 'Blessed are they whose transgressions are forgiven, whose sins are covered.

[8] Blessed is the man whose sin the Lord will never count against him.'

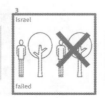

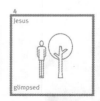

10. *How do these verses say we can be right with God?*

In Genesis 15:6 we read: 'Abram believed the LORD, and he credited it to him as righteousness'. Righteousness means 'being right with God' and justified means 'made right with God'. If God is going to create a new world for us then he must make us right with him. We need to be reconciled with God.

But how can God say that Abraham is in the right? Abraham is not in the right. Like all of us, Abraham keeps messing up.

11. *Why can't God just forgive us?*

God wants to forgive us and make us right with him even though we are guilty. But God is just and good and he must remain just and good in everything he does. If God overlooked our rebellion he would be acting as if the suffering we have caused did not matter. He must find a way to forgive us without ignoring what we have done. He must also find a way of giving us new hearts that love him and serve him.

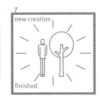

SUMMARY

God promises:

• a people who know God

• a land of plenty and security

God will restore our relationships with one another, with the environment and with himself.

BACKGROUND READING FOR THE NEXT SESSION

Nehemiah, chapter 9

We cannot create God's new world

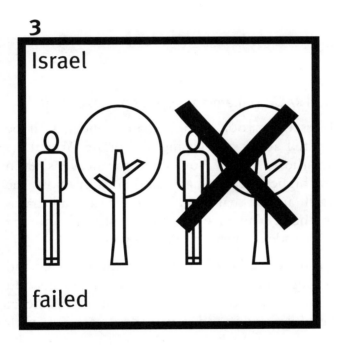

God set his people free and gave them a land
of plenty and security, but they could not
create God's new world. God promises that
he himself will put it right.

1. Can you think of attempts to create a perfect society?

2. Why do you think that these attempts so often fail?

BIBLE EXTRACT: Nehemiah, chapter 9, verses 5–8

Blessed be your glorious name, and may it be exalted above all blessing and praise. You alone are the LORD. ⁶ You made the heavens, even the highest heavens, and all their starry host, the earth and all that is on it, the seas and all that is in them. You give life to everything, and the multitudes of heaven worship you.

⁷ You are the LORD God, who chose Abram and brought him out of Ur of the Chaldeans and named him Abraham. ⁸ You found his heart faithful to you, and you made a covenant with him to give to his descendants the land of the Canaanites, Hittites, Amorites, Perizzites,

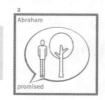

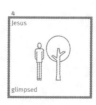

Jebusites and Girgashites. You have kept your promise because you are righteous.

God promised Abraham a new world. The Bible is the story of how God keeps that promise. This passage was spoken by the people of Israel (Abraham's descendants). It looks back over several hundred years of their history.

3. What did God promise Abraham (verses 7–8)?

4. Who is the God who made these promises to Abraham (verse 6)?

Abraham's family prospered and became a great nation (the nation of Israel) just as God promised (verse 8). They went to Egypt to escape famine. But as the years went by the nation of Egypt no longer welcomed them. Instead they made them slaves and oppressed them cruelly.

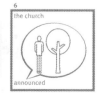
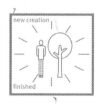

BIBLE EXTRACT: Nehemiah, chapter 9, verses 9–31

You saw the suffering of our forefathers in Egypt; you heard their cry at the Red Sea. ¹⁰ You sent miraculous signs and wonders against Pharaoh, against all his officials and all the people of his land, for you knew how arrogantly the Egyptians treated them. You made a name for yourself, which remains to this day. ¹¹ You divided the sea before them, so that they passed through it on dry ground, but you hurled their pursuers into the depths, like a stone into mighty waters. ¹² By day you led them with a pillar of cloud, and by night with a pillar of fire to give them light on the way they were to take.

¹³ You came down on Mount Sinai; you spoke to them from heaven. You gave them regulations and laws that are just and right, and decrees and commands that are good. ¹⁴ You made known to them your holy Sabbath and gave them commands, decrees and laws through your servant Moses. ¹⁵ In their hunger you gave them bread from heaven and in their thirst you brought them water from the rock; you told them to go in and take possession of the land you had sworn with uplifted hand to give them.

¹⁶ But they, our forefathers, became arrogant and stiff-necked, and did not obey your commands.

[17] They refused to listen and failed to remember the miracles you performed among them. They became stiff-necked and in their rebellion appointed a leader in order to return to their slavery. But you are a forgiving God, gracious and compassionate, slow to anger and abounding in love. Therefore you did not desert them, [18] even when they cast for themselves an image of a calf and said, 'This is your god, who brought you up out of Egypt,' or when they committed awful blasphemies.

[19] Because of your great compassion you did not abandon them in the desert. By day the pillar of cloud did not cease to guide them on their path, nor the pillar of fire by night to shine on the way they were to take. [20] You gave your good Spirit to instruct them. You did not withhold your manna from their mouths, and you gave them water for their thirst. [21] For forty years you sustained them in the desert; they lacked nothing, their clothes did not wear out nor did their feet become swollen.

[22] You gave them kingdoms and nations, allotting to them even the remotest frontiers. They took over the country of Sihon king of Heshbon and the country of Og king of Bashan. [23] You made their sons as numerous as the stars in the sky,

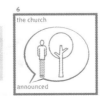

and you brought them into the land that you told their fathers to enter and possess. ²⁴ Their sons went in and took possession of the land. You subdued before them the Canaanites, who lived in the land; you handed the Canaanites over to them, along with their kings and the peoples of the land, to deal with them as they pleased. ²⁵ They captured fortified cities and fertile land; they took possession of houses filled with all kinds of good things, wells already dug, vineyards, olive groves and fruit trees in abundance. They ate to the full and were well-nourished; they revelled in your great goodness.

²⁶ But they were disobedient and rebelled against you; they put your law behind their backs. They killed your prophets, who had admonished them in order to turn them back to you; they committed awful blasphemies. ²⁷ So you handed them over to their enemies, who oppressed them. But when they were oppressed they cried out to you. From heaven you heard them, and in your great compassion you gave them deliverers, who rescued them from the hand of their enemies.

²⁸ But as soon as they were at rest, they again did what was evil in your sight. Then you abandoned them to the hand of their enemies so that they

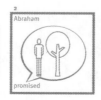

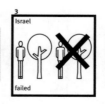

ruled over them. And when they cried out to you again, you heard from heaven, and in your compassion you delivered them time after time.

²⁹ You warned them to return to your law, but they became arrogant and disobeyed your commands. They sinned against your ordinances, by which a man will live if he obeys them. Stubbornly they turned their backs on you, became stiff-necked and refused to listen. ³⁰ For many years you were patient with them. By your Spirit you admonished them through your prophets. Yet they paid no attention, so you handed them over to the neighbouring peoples. ³¹ But in your great mercy you did not put an end to them or abandon them, for you are a gracious and merciful God.

5. *What did God do for Israel?*

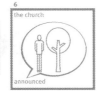
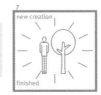

6. What does this show us about the character of God (verse 17)?

In Egypt God's people were not free to worship him and they were away from the land God had promised. But God sent miraculous disasters on Egypt to persuade the king of Egypt to let his people go free. God parted the Red Sea so that his people could escape the Egyptian army (verses 9–11). We call this 'the exodus' which means 'going out' or 'exit'. God had rescued his people *out* of Egypt. He had set them free.

God gave his people a set of laws (verses 13–14). Egyptian rule had been harsh and cruel. But God's law protected people from cruelty and made sure everyone was provided for. It was a rule of blessing, freedom and rest. God told his people that if they lived under his law, then the other nations would realise how good it was to live under God's rule. They would be attracted to God through the life of his people. The people would be a light to the nations.

7. How did the nation of Israel treat God (verses 16–18 and 26–31)?

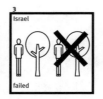
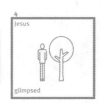

8. What does this show us about the character of human beings?

God had rescued his people and invited them to enjoy his blessing. But they did not trust God or obey him (verses 15–17). So God gave the land to the next generation through many remarkable victories (verses 22–27). But still the people did not trust God or obey him. They started to follow false gods with cruel practices. Instead of being a light to the nations, they were corrupted by the nations. Finally the people were exiled into Babylon and the land was captured.

BIBLE EXTRACT: Nehemiah, chapter 9, verses 32–37

> Now therefore, O our God, the great, mighty and awesome God, who keeps his covenant of love, do not let all this hardship seem trifling in your eyes – the hardship that has come upon us, upon our kings and leaders, upon our priests and prophets, upon our fathers and all your people, from the days of the kings of Assyria until today. [33] In all that has happened to us, you have been just; you have acted faithfully, while we did wrong. [34] Our kings, our leaders, our priests and our fathers did not follow your law; they did not pay attention to your commands or the warnings you

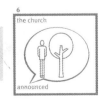

gave them. ³⁵ Even while they were in their kingdom, enjoying your great goodness to them in the spacious and fertile land you gave them, they did not serve you or turn from their evil ways.

³⁶ But see, we are slaves today, slaves in the land you gave our forefathers so that they could eat its fruit and the other good things it produces. ³⁷ Because of our sins, its abundant harvest goes to the kings you have placed over us. They rule over our bodies and our cattle as they please. We are in great distress.

9. How would you describe the mood of the people?

The nation of Israel is defeated. The land is owned by others. The people feel like slaves again – just as they were in Egypt. The people made a mess of living as God's people in God's land because they doubted his word and rejected his rule. We cannot create God's new world. Our dreams of utopia always fail. As we saw in the last session, if we are to be God's people and enjoy God's new world then God must deal with our rebellion and satisfy his judgment.

10. *In what ways are people today not free? What causes people to feel trapped?*

BIBLE EXTRACT: Ezekiel, chapter 36, verses 22–38

Therefore say to the house of Israel, 'This is what the Sovereign LORD says: It is not for your sake, O house of Israel, that I am going to do these things, but for the sake of my holy name, which you have profaned among the nations where you have gone. [23] I will show the holiness of my great name, which has been profaned among the nations, the name you have profaned among them. Then the nations will know that I am the LORD, declares the Sovereign LORD, when I show myself holy through you before their eyes.

[24] 'For I will take you out of the nations; I will gather you from all the countries and bring you back into your own land. [25] I will sprinkle clean water on you, and you will be clean; I will cleanse you from all your impurities and from all your idols. [26] I will give you a new heart and put a new spirit in you; I will remove from you your

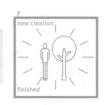

heart of stone and give you a heart of flesh.
²⁷ And I will put my Spirit in you and move you
to follow my decrees and be careful to keep my
laws. ²⁸ You will live in the land I gave your
forefathers; you will be my people, and I will be
your God. ²⁹ I will save you from all your
uncleanness. I will call for the corn and make it
plentiful and will not bring famine upon you. ³⁰ I
will increase the fruit of the trees and the crops
of the field, so that you will no longer suffer
disgrace among the nations because of famine…
³⁴ The desolate land will be cultivated instead of
lying desolate in the sight of all who pass
through it. ³⁵ They will say, "This land that was
laid waste has become like the garden of Eden;
the cities that were lying in ruins, desolate and
destroyed, are now fortified and inhabited."
³⁶ Then the nations around you that remain will
know that I the LORD have rebuilt what was
destroyed and have replanted what was desolate.
I the LORD have spoken, and I will do it.'

Ezekiel was a prophet who spoke to the Israelites exiled in
Babylon.

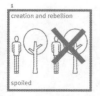
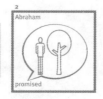

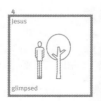

11. What was Ezekiel's message?

The people must have thought there was no hope left. But God promises to:

- rescue his people again (verse 24)
- make the land like a new garden of Eden (verses 30 and 35)

God also promises something greater: to deal with the problem of our hearts (verses 25–27). God will forgive us and remake us as new people.

Ezekiel also tells us *why* God will do this. It is not because we deserve to be rescued. In verse 23 God says that he will save us to show how great and how loving he is; to bring himself glory and worship. In our next session we will look at *how* God does this.

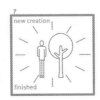

SUMMARY

God set his people free and gave them a good land of plenty and security. But they could not create God's new world. Nor could they escape the problem of God's judgment. But God will put it right through his promised rescuer.

BACKGROUND READING FOR THE NEXT SESSION

Mark, chapter 15, verse 1 to chapter 16, verse 8

Wedding

7:30 → 8 Make costumes
8 → 8:15 Ceremony   1Cor 13 v 1-8a.
8:15 → 8:40 Champagne reception
            + photos.
8:40 on Talk.
Decide next week - cinema
                  - Haugh Hill
                  - river
                  - ?

Middle names.

Dearly beloved....
Reading
Vows + RINGS!
Pronounce man + wife. Kiss the bride.
Celebration.

We can enjoy God's new world because of Jesus

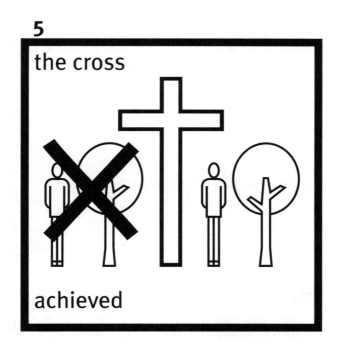

The death of Jesus deals with the problem of
rebellion and judgment. The resurrection of
Jesus is the promise and beginning
of God's new world.

THE WORLD WE ALL WANT

We have seen that as a result of our rejection of God:

- we have become God's enemies
- we have spoiled God's world

But God promises a new world and Jesus gave us a glimpse of God's new world. He healed the sick, raised the dead and fed the hungry. Yet the hope of a new world appeared to end when Jesus was killed. In this session we discover why it is that the death of Jesus is good news.

1. What gives you hope for the future?

2. What worries do you have about the future?

Read.

BIBLE EXTRACT: Mark, chapter 15, verses 22–39

> They brought Jesus to the place called Golgotha (which means The Place of the Skull). ²³ Then they offered him wine mixed with myrrh, but he

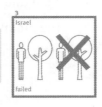
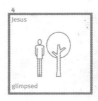

did not take it. ²⁴ And they crucified him. Dividing up his clothes, they cast lots to see what each would get.

²⁵ It was the third hour when they crucified him. ²⁶ The written notice of the charge against him read: THE KING OF THE JEWS. ²⁷ They crucified two robbers with him, one on his right and one on his left. ²⁹ Those who passed by hurled insults at him, shaking their heads and saying, 'So! You who are going to destroy the temple and build it in three days, ³⁰ come down from the cross and save yourself!'

³¹ In the same way the chief priests and the teachers of the law mocked him among themselves. 'He saved others,' they said, 'but he can't save himself! ³² Let this Christ, this King of Israel, come down now from the cross, that we may see and believe.' Those crucified with him also heaped insults on him.

³³ At the sixth hour darkness came over the whole land until the ninth hour. ³⁴ And at the ninth hour Jesus cried out in a loud voice, '*Eloi, Eloi, lama sabachthani?*' – which means, 'My God, my God, why have you forsaken me?'

³⁵ When some of those standing near heard this, they said, 'Listen, he's calling Elijah.'

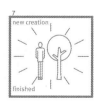

³⁶ One man ran, filled a sponge with wine vinegar, put it on a stick, and offered it to Jesus to drink. 'Now leave him alone. Let's see if Elijah comes to take him down,' he said.

³⁷ With a loud cry, Jesus breathed his last.

³⁸ The curtain of the temple was torn in two from top to bottom. ³⁹ And when the centurion, who stood there in front of Jesus, heard his cry and saw how he died, he said, 'Surely this man was the Son of God!'

'Christ' means 'anointed One'. Israel's kings were anointed with oil. The 'Christ' is God's promised rescuer and King. Throughout the story God has repeatedly promised someone who will rescue us. Mark has portrayed Jesus as that promised rescuer, as the hero of the story.

3. What do the religious leaders think about Jesus (verses 29–32)? *What do they think will happen.*

4. Who does the Roman soldier think Jesus is (verse 39)?

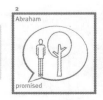
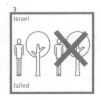
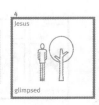

The religious leaders think the true Christ will save God's people by coming down from the cross. But Jesus said it was *necessary* for him to die (see Mark 8:31). Jesus is God's promised rescuer. He is the hero of the story. And he saves us by staying on the cross.

5. What happens when Jesus dies (verses 33–34)?

What do you think forsaken means?

*separated
deserted
forgotten
about*

6. Did Jesus deserve to die forsaken by God?

So why did it have to happen

*— last week God just punishment 4 sin
jesus in love took punishment.*

7. The curtain of the temple kept people from the holiest part of the temple – the symbol of God's presence. What do you think is the significance of the curtain being torn in two as Jesus dies (verse 38)?

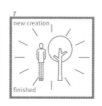

When Jesus dies the land becomes dark and he is forsaken by God. We spoiled God's world – now there is darkness over the land. We became God's enemies – now Jesus is abandoned by God.

The death of Jesus was no ordinary death. Jesus died *for us*. He did not deserve to be forsaken by God – he had only done good. We are the ones who deserve to be forsaken by God. We deserve to be punished for our rebellion against God and the way we have spoiled his world. But Jesus died in our place as our substitute. In this way Jesus deals with the problem of God's judgment against us. Jesus took our punishment and curse. God abandoned Jesus so that we would not have to be abandoned. As a result we can be free to enjoy God's new world.

8. What are the things people think they must do to be right with God?

When Jesus died the curtain was torn into two. It is a picture of an open door into God's kingdom. God welcomes anyone who wants to come to him. Jesus has done everything needed to make us right with God.

BIBLE EXTRACT: Mark, chapter 16, verses 1–8

When the Sabbath was over, Mary Magdalene,

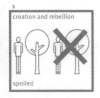

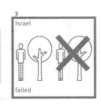
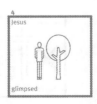

Mary the mother of James, and Salome bought spices so that they might go to anoint Jesus' body. ² Very early on the first day of the week, just after sunrise, they were on their way to the tomb ³ and they asked each other, 'Who will roll the stone away from the entrance of the tomb?'

⁴ But when they looked up, they saw that the stone, which was very large, had been rolled away. ⁵ As they entered the tomb, they saw a young man dressed in a white robe sitting on the right side, and they were alarmed.

⁶ 'Don't be alarmed,' he said. 'You are looking for Jesus the Nazarene, who was crucified. He has risen! He is not here. See the place where they laid him. ⁷ But go, tell his disciples and Peter, "He is going ahead of you into Galilee. There you will see him, just as he told you."'

⁸ Trembling and bewildered, the women went out and fled from the tomb. They said nothing to anyone, because they were afraid.

9. *What do the women find when they go to the tomb?*

Stone rolled away
Young man in white robe

what would they say happened.

Some people say that Jesus never really died – that he fainted on the cross. But one of the Roman soldiers made sure he was dead and he was buried in a sealed tomb (see Mark 15:44–46). Some people suggest that his followers stole his body to prove his claims. But guards were put on the tomb (see Matthew 27:62–66 and 28:11–15) and later his followers were prepared to die for the truth of the resurrection. The explanation of the empty tomb which the Bible gives is that Jesus rose from the dead.

10. *What do you make of the claim that Jesus rose from the dead?*

11. *What difference do you think it makes if Jesus rose from the dead?*

God's promise that death defeated.
Cross was

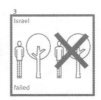

The resurrection of Jesus is God's promise that death is defeated. The man at the tomb says it is the *crucified* one who has been raised (Mark 16:6). It is the one who died as a result of God's judgment who has now been raised by God. So the resurrection is God's way of saying the cross was a success. Jesus has dealt with our rebellion and he has overcome death. The resurrection is the promise and the beginning of God's new world.

If Jesus rose from the dead what response does he want from us? If his promise of a new world can be trusted, how can we be part of that new world? We will consider these questions in our next session.

SUMMARY

The death of Jesus deals with the problem of rebellion and judgment. The resurrection of Jesus is the promise and beginning of God's new world.

BACKGROUND READING FOR THE NEXT SESSION

Acts, chapters 1–2

Christians are God's people waiting for God's new world

6

the church

announced

Jesus sent the Holy Spirit to help us be God's
new people while we wait for God's new world.
We become God's people through
faith and repentance.

1. *What do people in our society think being a Christian means?*

We have seen that God promises a new world and that Jesus died in our place so that we can enjoy it. The next Bible extract describes what happened a few days after Jesus rose from the dead.

BIBLE EXTRACT: Acts, chapter 1, verses 6–11

> So when the followers of Jesus met together, they asked Jesus, 'Lord, are you at this time going to restore the kingdom to Israel?'
>
> 7 He said to them: 'It is not for you to know the times or dates the Father has set by his own authority. 8 But you will receive power when the Holy Spirit comes on you; and you will be my witnesses in Jerusalem, and in all Judea and Samaria, and to the ends of the earth.'
>
> 9 After he said this, he was taken up before their very eyes, and a cloud hid him from their sight.
>
> 10 They were looking intently up into the sky as he was going, when suddenly two men dressed in

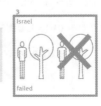

white stood beside them. ¹¹ 'Men of Galilee,' they said, 'why do you stand here looking into the sky? This same Jesus, who has been taken from you into heaven, will come back in the same way you have seen him go into heaven.'

2. What are Christians waiting for (verse 11)?

3. What is the job Jesus gives to his followers?

4. Where are Christians to tell the good news of God's coming world?

Christians are people waiting for Jesus to come back and create God's new world. This is good news. Jesus invites us to be part of

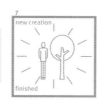

God's new world. He also invites us to tell other people this good news. Jesus sends us out as his witnesses to tell all nations. God will bless all nations as he promised Abraham (Genesis 12:3). And Jesus gives us the Holy Spirit to help us. The Holy Spirit is God with us. He gives us a new ability to serve God (as God promised in Ezekiel 36:25–27). Christians are the first to admit we are not all we should be. We often do not live as we should. These failures make us long even more for Jesus to return.

BIBLE EXTRACT: Acts, chapter 2, verses 14, 22–24 and 32–47

Then Peter stood up with the Eleven, raised his voice and addressed the crowd: '...Men of Israel, listen to this: Jesus of Nazareth was a man accredited by God to you by miracles, wonders and signs, which God did among you through him, as you yourselves know. 23 This man was handed over to you by God's set purpose and foreknowledge; and you, with the help of wicked men, put him to death by nailing him to the cross. 24 But God raised him from the dead, freeing him from the agony of death, because it was impossible for death to keep its hold on him … God has raised this Jesus to life, and we are all witnesses of the fact. 33 Exalted to the right hand of God, he has received from the Father the promised Holy Spirit and has poured out what you now see and hear. 34 For David did not

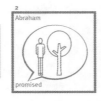

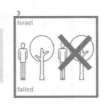

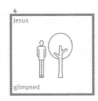

ascend to heaven, and yet he said, "The Lord said to my Lord: 'Sit at my right hand ³⁵ until I make your enemies a footstool for your feet.'"

³⁶ 'Therefore let all Israel be assured of this: God has made this Jesus, whom you crucified, both Lord and Christ.'

³⁷ When the people heard this, they were cut to the heart and said to Peter and the other apostles, 'Brothers, what shall we do?'

³⁸ Peter replied, 'Repent and be baptised, every one of you, in the name of Jesus Christ for the forgiveness of your sins. And you will receive the gift of the Holy Spirit. ³⁹ The promise is for you and your children and for all who are far off – for all whom the Lord our God will call.'

⁴⁰ With many other words he warned them; and he pleaded with them, 'Save yourselves from this corrupt generation.' ⁴¹ Those who accepted his message were baptised, and about three thousand were added to their number that day.

⁴² They devoted themselves to the apostles' teaching and to the fellowship, to the breaking of bread and to prayer. ⁴³ Everyone was filled with awe, and many wonders and miraculous signs

were done by the apostles. ⁴⁴ All the believers were together and had everything in common. ⁴⁵ Selling their possessions and goods, they gave to anyone as he had need. ⁴⁶ Every day they continued to meet together in the temple courts. They broke bread in their homes and ate together with glad and sincere hearts, ⁴⁷ praising God and enjoying the favour of all the people. And the Lord added to their number daily those who were being saved.

5. Who does Peter say that Jesus is (verse 36)?

6. How do people become part of God's community (see verse 38)?

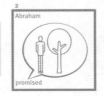
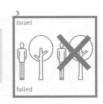
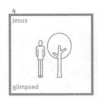

7. *What is promised to members of God's community (see verses 38–39)?*

When we become part of God's people our rebellion is forgiven and we receive a new relationship with him through his Spirit. What was promised long ago to Abraham is for us. Instead of being God's enemies we can know God and instead of a spoiled world we can look forward to his new world.

8. *What is God's community to be like?*

Christians are people who are committed to one another, share together and love one another as Jesus has loved us (see verses 42–47). This means the church is the prototype of the world we all want. Just as Jesus gave us a glimpse of that world in his life so his people are a foretaste of what is to come.

We have seen that Christians are:

- a waiting community
- a proclaiming community
- a loving community

When the people asked Peter what they must do to become part of God's new world he said: '*Repent and be baptised, every one of you, in the name of Jesus Christ for the forgiveness of your sins*' (verse 38). We become God's people through repentance and faith.

Repentance

Repentance means turning back to God. It means recognising our part in spoiling this world and accepting God's new world with God in control. We give up our membership of the community that rejects God. We become members of the community that loves God and serves Jesus.

Faith

Baptism is a symbolic act that involves being covered with water. It is a picture of faith in what God has done for us. Faith means believing the promise of God. It means trusting Jesus to rescue us through his death and resurrection. We need to recognise that Jesus is our only hope – there's nothing we can do to help save ourselves.

The big question is: is God's new world the world you want? Do you want a world in which God is in control? God's good world was spoiled when we rejected God. Now God offers you a place in his new world. But you will only enjoy it if you turn back to God and trust in Jesus. Peter urged the people: '*save yourselves*' (verse 40). If you continue to live without Christ then you will face God's terrible judgment. If you want to be part of God's new world then you must turn to Jesus with repentance and faith. You must show it in baptism as you become part of his new family. We can work together to create a glimpse of God's new world and together we

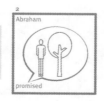
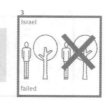

can look forward to the day when it comes in all its wonderful glory. Will you turn from being at the centre of your world, and accept Jesus as your Lord and trust him as your rescuer?

9. What, if anything, is stopping you becoming a Christian?

SUMMARY

Jesus sent the Holy Spirit to help us be God's new people while we wait for God's new world. We become God's people through faith and repentance.

FOR LEADERS

We all dream of a better world – a world of security, plenty and friendship. Christians believe that God promises just such a new world. The Bible is the story of God making that promise and keeping it. *The World We All Want* is for people who are interested in the message of the Bible. It is an introduction to the Bible story – the story Christians believe to be the story of our world and its future. The course has been used with people of different nationalities, different social backgrounds and different ages. It has been through many revisions and we are grateful to people within the Crowded House network of churches and beyond for all their ideas and feedback.

THE DISTINCTIVES

A point of connection

The course begins by exploring the idea of 'the world we all want'. This provides a natural point of contact with people; a common aspiration. It establishes at the beginning of the course a reason why the Bible story is so important. As the course develops, however, it makes it clear that this world cannot be human-centred – it must be God-centred.

The Bible story

The World We All Want presents the gospel through the Bible story. We have found other courses assume too much background knowledge of the Bible. *The World We All Want* presents the biblical view of the world that people need if they are to understand the work of Christ. Moreover retelling the Bible story offers an engaging way of presenting the gospel to people today.

A community

Often contemporary presentations of the gospel are individualistic. They focus on an individual's relationship with God. It then becomes difficult to teach people about the church except in functional terms or terms that contradict the message of grace. The focus of the Bible, however, is on God's plan to create a people who are his people. *The World We All Want* focuses on the communal nature of the gospel in a way that naturally integrates the church into the message of the gospel.

THE FORMAT

We hope you will find the course flexible and encourage you to adapt it to suit your needs. We have designed the material with two formats in mind:

1. As a one-to-one or small group Bible study. Work through the Bible studies with people, reading the Bible passages together, looking at the questions, reading the summary paragraphs and answering people's questions as you go along. The inclusion of prose summaries should make the material self-explanatory so that new Christians can use it with their friends. The material can even be used by someone on their own.

2. With a larger group working in small groups on the Bible study and coming together for a talk. This is the format made popular by *The Alpha Course* from Holy Trinity Brompton and *Christianity Explored* from All Souls, Langham Place. Sample talks are available on *The World We All Want* website – www.thecrowdedhouse.org/twwaw. *The World We All Want* could also be used as baptism or confirmation classes.

The Bible study is based on, but not dependent on, a passage that participants have been asked to read (with the exception of the first session). Each session ends with a 'teaser' that sets up the issues to be considered in the following session.

- Encourage people to ask questions and answer their questions with respect and honesty. If you do not know an answer then say so.

- Give time to building relationships with people so they can see what Christianity looks like in practice as they get to know you and so that discussions can be more open. Combining each session with a meal provides a great context in which this can happen.

- Encourage people to share their opinions and responses. You may want to ask people at the end of each session how they think what you have been talking about relates to them.

- Introduce people to your Christian friends so they can see Christian relationships and Christian community.

- Encourage people to read the Bible for themselves so they explore the Bible rather than your opinions.

- You can simply read out loud the explanations in each study, but you might like to put them into your own words or illustrate them from your own experience.

Some questions are designed to create discussion (often phrased 'what do you think?' or 'what do people think?'). The purpose of these questions is to open up discussion and enable people to contribute at an equal level. Do not worry about getting a 'correct' answer. Other questions are about the text. Try to ensure people understand the correct answer. It is best to do this by pointing them to the text of the Bible rather than answering the question for them.

The World We All Want has been designed so it can be used with other courses like *Christianity Explored*. *The World We All Want* has been written for people with little background knowledge of the Bible so it may be better to start with it and then move on to other courses. *The World We All Want* uses passages from Mark's Gospel in its discussion of Jesus to help people who might do, or who have done, *Christianity Explored* make the connections between the story of Jesus and the Bible story as a whole.

THE TALKS

Sample talks are available on *The World We All Want* website – www.thecrowdedhouse.org/twwaw. The talks are designed to pull ideas together and add further explanations and illustrations. Some people may want to use the talks as they are, but we encourage people to adapt them and make them their own. Leaders who are just doing a Bible study may still find it helpful to read through the talks in preparation as they may provide explanations and illustrations that can be used in discussion as appropriate.

A good way to introduce *The World We All Want* to your church or Christian Union is to preach through it or run it among your home groups. This will help people appreciate the good news of the Bible story and get them familiar with the ideas in the course. It could also provide an opportunity to invite friends as a way of introducing them to the course.

THE PICTURES

The person in the pictures represents a new people and the tree represents a new land or a new earth. These are the two features of God's promise that are highlighted throughout in the course. They have been designed so that anyone can draw them for themselves. You can use the summaries of each session to explain the pictures.

THE OUTLINE

SESSION ONE
Title: God promises the world we all want
Bible Passages: Revelation 21–22 and Mark 5
Diagram: No. 7 New creation
Summary: *God promises the world we all want. We know
                     this promise is real because there was a point in
                     history when we glimpsed the world we all
                     want.*

SESSION TWO
Title: Jesus shows us God's new world
Bible Passages: Mark 4–5 and Mark 8
Diagram: No. 4 Jesus
Summary: *Jesus had the power to make God's new
                     world. But Jesus said it was necessary for him
                     to die so we could enjoy it.*

SESSION THREE
Title: We have spoiled God's good world
Bible Passages: Genesis 1–3
Diagram: No. 1 Creation and rebellion
Summary: *We have spoiled the good world that God
                     made, but God promises someone who will
                     put it right.*

SESSION FOUR
Title: God promises a new world
Bible Passages: Genesis 12 and 15 and Romans 4
Diagram: No. 2 Abraham
Summary: *God promises a people who know God and a
                     land of plenty and security.*

SESSION FIVE

Title: We cannot create God's new world
Bible Passages: Nehemiah 9 and Ezekiel 36
Diagram: No. 3 Israel
Summary: *God set his people free and gave them a land
                       of plenty and security, but they could not
                       create God's new world. God promises that
                       he himself will put it right.*

SESSION SIX

Title: We can enjoy God's new world because of
                       Jesus
Bible Passages: Mark 15–16
Diagram: No. 5 The cross
Summary: *The death of Jesus deals with the problem of
                       rebellion and judgment. The resurrection of
                       Jesus is the promise and beginning of God's
                       new world.*

SESSION SEVEN

Title: Christians are God's people waiting for God's
                       new world
Bible Passages: Acts 1–2
Diagram: No. 6 The church
Summary: *Jesus sent the Holy Spirit to help us be God's
                       new people while we wait for God's new
                       world. We become God's people through faith
                       and repentance.*

It is possible to run the course in five or six sessions:

Combine sessions one and two by moving from the end of session one to the Mark 8 reading in session two.

Combine sessions three and four by replacing question 11 in session three with the reading from Genesis 12:1–7 and questions 3–5 in session four.

Further Reading

From Creation to New Creation: Understanding the Bible Story

Tim Chester

Large parts of the Bible are unfamiliar territory for many people. We're not sure what to make of them, still less how to live by them. *From Creation To New Creation* gives us a route map. By tracing the unfolding promises of God, it enables us to make sense of the Bible story. The result is a book that not only shows us how to understand the Bible as a whole, but also how it continues to speak to people in the twenty-first century.

'*Have you ever wondered how the whole Bible fits together? Here is the help you need. An easy-to-read style and great diagrams show how God's promises unfold through the Bible story and how they apply to us. The way you read the Bible will never be quite the same again.*'
Julian Hardyman, Eden Baptist Church, Cambridge

'*For many, reading the Bible is like getting lost in a maze. We explore all sorts of avenues, take misleading short cuts, explore dead ends and never reach the destination. Tim Chester knows the importance of providing the big map. He proves a reliable guide, using his clear and straightforward communication skills.*'
Derek Tidball, Principal of London Bible College

Tim Chester is part of a church planting project in Sheffield and co-author of *The World We All Want*.

ISBN 1-84227-204-7

PATERNOSTER PRESS
Available from your local Christian bookshop or
www.authenticmedia.co.uk

Turning Points

Vaughan Roberts

Is there meaning to life? Is human history a random process going nowhere? Or is it under control – heading towards a goal, a destination? And what about my life? Where do I fit into the grand scheme of things?

These are topical questions in any age, but perhaps particularly so in a largely disillusioned postmodern era such as ours. Vaughan Roberts addresses these questions and others as he looks at what the Bible presents as the 'turning points' in history, from creation to the end of the world.

This book does not read like a normal history book. No mention is made of the great battles and emperors of whom we learnt at school. It will not help you pass exams or score extra marks in a pub quiz.

It aims to do something far more important to help you see history as God sees it, so that you might fit in with his plans for the world.

'*Racy and profound, brilliant and biblical, this book is a powerful apologetic and magnet to Jesus Christ. Vaughan gets right inside contemporary emptiness and despair and speaks good news into it with charm and clarity.*' Michael Green, Advisor in Evangelism to the Archbishops of Canterbury and York

'*If Christianity seems alien or inaccessible to you, this book is for you. Vaughan Roberts outlines some of the major 'turning points' of the Bible. Better yet, he does so in an attractive way that is free of jargon. I warmly recommend it.*' Don Carson, Trinity Evangelical Divinity School

Vaughan Roberts is the Rector of St Ebbe's Church, Oxford.

ISBN 1-8507-8336-5

AUTHENTIC
Available from your local Christian bookshop or
www.authenticmedia.co.uk